Early Blues, Ancient Ballads, and Classic Folk Songs for
Fingerstyle Guitar

by Glenn Weiser

To access audio visit:
www.halleonard.com/mylibrary

Enter Code
4785-9161-1175-8248

ISBN 978-1-57424-386-4
SAN 683-8022

Cover by James Creative Group

Front and back cover guitar: Zogbaum and Fairchild guitar, ca. 1860-68, with William B. Tilton's patent improvements. The silver medallion in the soundhole is mounted on the patented dowel that Tilton built into his instruments, and the strings go through, not over, the bridge. The tailpiece is not original. The silver medallion reads "Wm. B. Tilton's Improvement, New York, Patented 1857."

Copyright © 2019 CENTERSTREAM Publishing
P.O. Box 17878 - Anaheim Hills, CA 92817

www.centerstream-usa.com | centerstrm@aol.com | 714-779-9390

1875 Cabinet card.

Table of Contents

This book is respectfully dedicated to

the memory of my late father-in-law,

Salvatore J. Pomelitto

Introduction

This book is a collection of twenty-five fingerstyle guitar arrangements of famous early blues, centuries-old ballads, and traditional folk songs. These songs have been covered by rock, pop, folk, and country bands and artists such as The Animals, Joan Baez, The Beach Boys, The Byrds, Bob Dylan, Johnny Cash, Judy Collins, The Grateful Dead, Woody Guthrie, Emmylou Harris, George Jones, The Kingston Trio, Peter, Paul & Mary, Pete Seeger, Simon and Garfunkel, James Taylor, Traffic, Dave Van Ronk, and others.

The arrangements are ideal for the singer-guitarist or accompanist who wants to play a melodic fingerstyle solo break between the verses of a song, but they also can be enjoyed on their own or paired into medleys. They include standard notation with fingering, tablature, guitar chords, lyrics, header notes, and online audio. These songs fall into three categories.

First, there are four of the oldest known blues songs. No one knows exactly when and where in the South the blues began, but Jelly Roll Morton (1890-1941) said they had been played in New Orleans for as long as anyone could remember. "Buddy Bolden's Blues" and "Careless Love" were popularized, if not composed, by Buddy Bolden, the Crescent City cornetist who led the first jazz band in the opening years of the twentieth century. "St. James Infirmary," another 'Nawlins' tune, and "C. C. Rider" are also among the earliest blues.

Next, there are several narrative ballads, some dating back centuries, Celtic love songs, and a sea shanty from the British Isles. "Barbara Allen," "The Golden Vanity," "The House Carpenter," "Scarborough Fair," are all Child ballads, which are the oldest known Anglo-Scottish songs as collected and edited by Prof. Francis Child (1825-1896) of Harvard University in the late 1800s. The melody of "The Last Rose of Summer" is a lovely Irish harp tune, and "Loch Lomond" is a famous Scottish song. "Jack Tar the Sailor" is a sea shanty with a modal melody that evokes the rolling waves of the ocean.

Lastly, there are several American folk songs. "John Henry" is probably the best-known American hero ballad. "Wildwood Flower," "Will the Circle Be Unbroken," and "Bury Me Beneath the Willow" were recorded by the Carter Family during the years 1927-1935 and became country music standards. "We Shall Overcome," a hymn that was adopted as a labor song, became the anthem of the civil rights movement. "Shenandoah" is a strikingly beautiful old love song from the rivers of the upper Mississippi basin.

The guitar arrangements here fall into different categories: alternate-thumb Travis picking, blues and ragtime, classical guitar style, slow ballads with arpeggiated bass lines, etc. You can always use a capo or drop the tuning of the guitar by a whole step if you need to change the key of a song.

After the lyrics of each song I have listed some recommended versions on YouTube that you can listen to. Just search by title and artist. Singers can study the vocal stylings also.

Lastly, if you'd like help learning these pieces, I offer private guitar lessons on Skype/FaceTime. Visit my website at www.celticguitarmusic.com for details.

Enjoy the music!

Glenn Weiser
Southwick, MA
August 2019

The Banks of the Ohio

This American folk song is descended from an 18th-century English ballad, "The Oxford Girl," and is found in variants as "The Wexford Girl" and "The Knoxville Girl." Willie walks by the Ohio River with his sweetheart and proposes marriage. When she silenty spurns him, he stabs her and throws her in the river. The lyrics were first collected in 1915, and the song was recorded in 1927 by Grayson and Whitter as "I'll Never Be Yours."

American folk song

Arr. G. Weiser

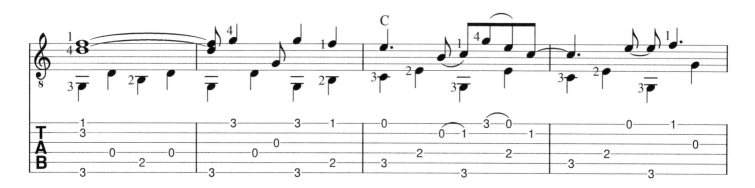

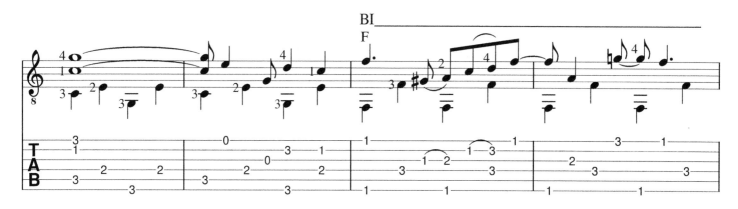

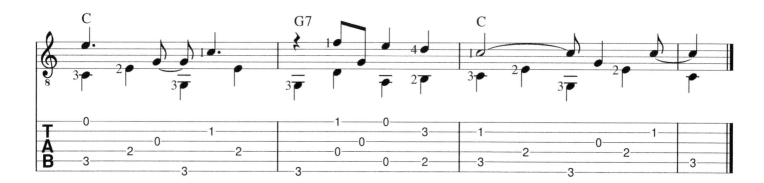

The Banks of the Ohio

I asked my love to take a walk,
Just a walk a little way,
And as we walked, we began to talk,
All about our wedding day.

Chorus:
    Only say that you'll be mine,
    In no other's arms entwine,
    Down beside where the waters flow,
    Down by the banks of the Ohio.

I asked her to become my wife,
And I'd live happy all my life,
Not a word did she say,
She only rose and turned away.
(chorus)

I held a knife against her breast,
As into my arms she pressed,
She said "Oh, Willie, don't you murder me,
I'm unprepared for eternity."
(chorus)

I took her by her lily-white hand,
And dragged her down that bank of sand,
There I threw her in to drown,
I watched her as she floated down.
(chorus)

As I walked home twixt twelve and one,
Thinking of what I had done,
I killed the girl I love you see,
Because she would not marry me.
(chorus)

The very next day twixt three and four,
Sheriff Brown knocked on my door,
He said "Young man, don't you try to run,
You have to pay for what you've done."
(chorus)

Recommended versions on YouTube: Joan Baez, Johnny Cash, Tony Rice.

Barbara Allen (Child 84)

This is among the most famous Child ballads, and has been recorded or performed in concert by Bob Dylan, Joan Baez, Judy Collins, Pete Seeger, and many other folksingers. First mentioned by the English diarist and naval official Samuel Pepys in 1666 as a "little Scotch song," its lyrics tell of a rejected suitor who, spurned by "hardhearted Barbara Allen," dies of grief. Overcome with remorse, she too dies and they are buried side by side. A rose and a briar grow from their graves and intertwine, symbolizing in a striking image the union that was never consummated in life. You can hear this in the 1938 film version of *A Christmas Carol* when a transformed Ebenezer Scrooge stops by the home of Bob Crachit as the family is singing at the piano.

Traditional Scottish ballad

Arr. G. Weiser

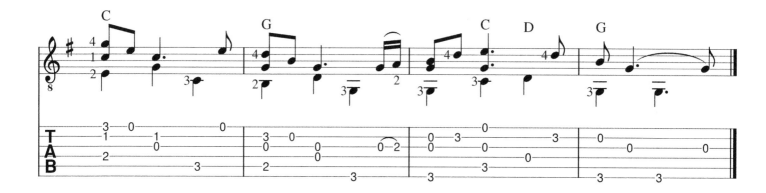

Bob Dylan.

Barbara Allen

'Twas in the merry month of May,
When green buds all were swelling,
Sweet William on his death bed lay,
For love of Barbara Allen.

He sent his servant to the town,
To the place where she was dwelling,
Saying "You must come, to my master dear,
If your name be Barbara Allen."

So slowly, slowly she got up.
And slowly she drew nigh him,
And the only words to him did say,
"Young man, I think you're dying."

He turned his face unto the wall,
And death was in him welling,
"Good-bye, good-bye, to my friends all,
Be good to Barbara Allen."

When he was dead and laid in grave,
She heard the death bells knelling,
And every stroke to her did say,
"Hard hearted Barbara Allen."

"Oh mother, mother, dig my grave,
Make it both long and narrow,
Sweet William died of love for me,
And I will die of sorrow."

"And father, father, dig my grave,
Make it both long and narrow,
Sweet William died on yesterday,
And I will die tomorrow."

Barbara Allen was buried in the old churchyard,
Sweet William was buried beside her,
Out of sweet William's heart, there grew a rose,
Out of Barbara Allen's a briar.

They grew and grew in the old churchyard,
Till they could grow no higher,
At the end they formed, a true lover's knot,
And the rose grew round the briar.

Recommended versions on YouTube: A Christmas Carol (movie excerpt), Crystal Gayle.

Buddy Bolden's Blues

Although Wynton Marsalis credits this 16-bar blues as being the first jazz song, its precise origins are a subject of debate. According to Jelly Roll Morton, Charles "Buddy" Bolden (1877-1931), the New Orleans cornetist who led the first Dixieland band, wrote it in 1902. Bolden's trombonist, Willy Cornish, also claimed authorship. But the melody was published in the 1899 song "Cakewalk in the Sky," and again in the 1904 piano rag "The St. Louis Tickle." As the lyrics (which are also derivative) mention a "funky butt," it was considered rude to even whistle it on the streets of Storyville, the Crescent City's red-light district where jazz was born.

Traditional blues

Arr. G. Weiser

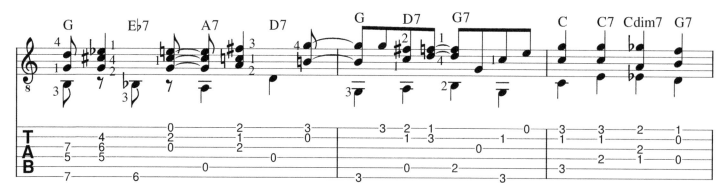

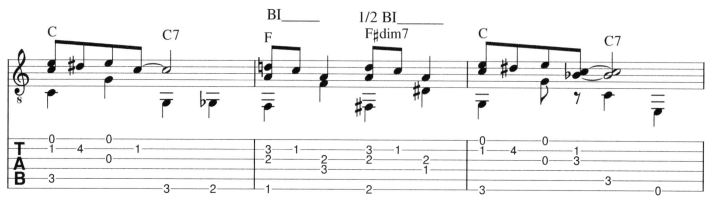

Copyright 2019 G Weiser

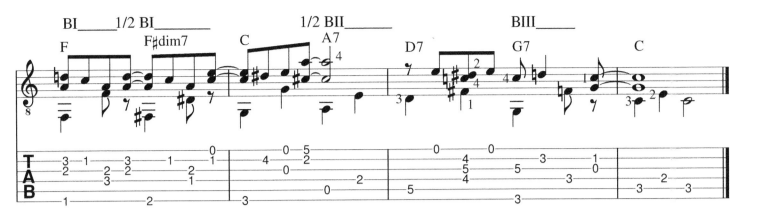

Buddy Bolden's Blues

I thought I heard Buddy Bolden say,
"Stinky butt, funky butt, take it away.
Stinky butt, funky butt, take it away,"
I thought I heard him say,
I thought I heard Buddy Bolden shout,
"Open up a window, and let that bad air out,
Open up a window, and let that foul air out,"
I thought I heard him shout.

I thought I heard Judge Fogarty say,
"Give him thirty days in the market, take him away,
Give him a good broom to sweep with, take him away,"
I thought I heard him say,
I thought I heard Frankie Duson shout,
"Gal, give me that money or I'm gonna beat it out,
Gal, give me that money or I'm gonna beat it out,"
I thought I heard him shout.

Recommended versions on YouTube: Jelly Roll Morton, Dave Van Ronk, Dr. John.

Buddy Bolden, (standing second from right) and his band, in the early 1890s. He was the epic hero not only of trumpet players but also of blues-oriented instrumentalists and dance–band leaders as well.

Bury Me Beneath the Willow

Thought to be descended from a 19th-century parlor song, this country and bluegrass standard was first published in 1909 by H. M. Belden in his *Ballads and Songs Collected by the Missouri Folk-Lore Society.* Henry Whitter, a millhand from Fries, Virginia, first recorded it in 1923. But the Carter Family, who had known the song since their childhood, made the lament for lost love famous with their 1927 version. I found the variant arranged here in *Albert E. Brumley's America's Memory Valley*, an old-time songbook.

American folk song

Arr. G. Weiser

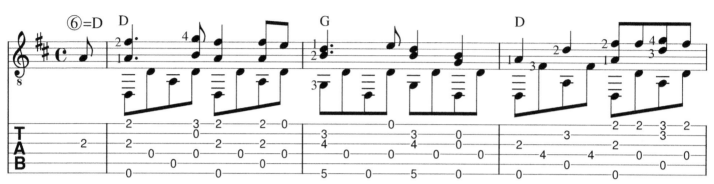

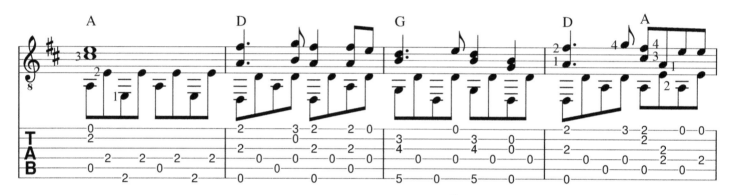

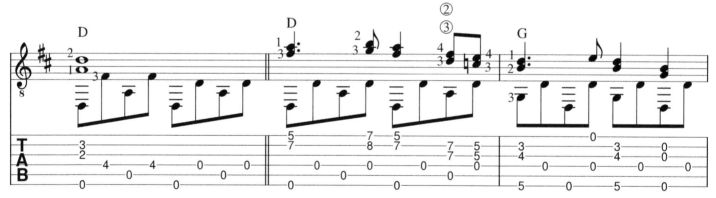

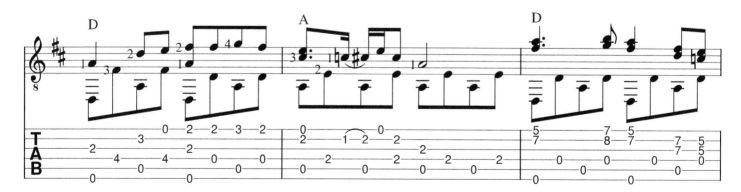

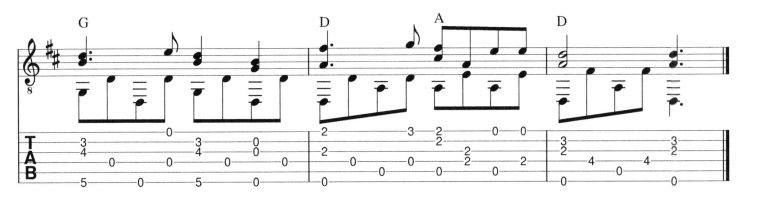

Bury Me Beneath the Willow

My heart is sad and I'm in sorrow,
For the only one I love,
When shall I see him? Oh, no, never,
Till I meet him in heaven above.

Chorus:
Oh, bury me beneath the willow,
Under the weeping willow tree.
So he may know where I am sleeping,
And perhaps he'll weep for me.

They told me that he did not love me,
I could not believe it was true,
Until an angel softly whispered,
He is proving untrue to you.
(chorus)

Tomorrow was to be our wedding,
But, O Lord, where can he be?
He has left me to court another,
And he cares no more for me.
(chorus)

Oh, bury me under the violets blue,
To prove my love to him,
Tell him that I would die to save him,
For his love I never could win.
(chorus)

Recommended versions on YouTube: The Carter Family, Skaggs and Rice, Bluegrass All-Stars.

C. C. Rider

In his 1927 *American Song Bag*, Carl Sandburg writes of this traditional blues, "John Lomax and I heard this song in Austin, Texas, in an old saloon, The Silver King, operated as a soft drink parlor by a Mexican negro, Martinez." He adds that 'C. C. Rider' is probably a variant of 'easy rider', a term for a loose woman. It was first recorded in 1924 as "See See Rider" by Gertrude "Ma" Rainey, and later by many others.

Traditional blues
Swing 8ths

Arr. G. Weiser

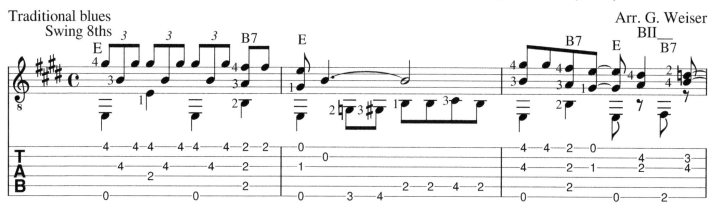

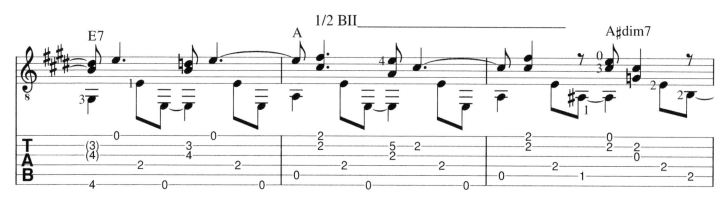

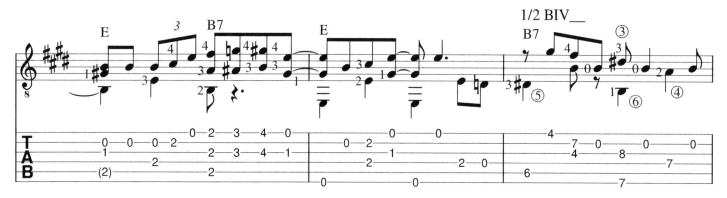

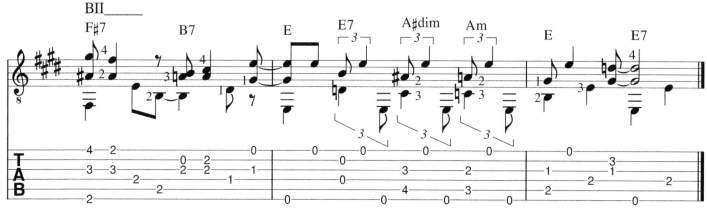

C.C. Rider

C.C. Rider, see what you have done, Lord, Lord, Lord,
C.C. Rider, see what you have done, Lord, Lord, Lord,
Well, you made me love you, now your man has come.

C.C. Rider, where did you stay last night, Lord, Lord, Lord,
C. C. where did you stay last night.
You come home this mornin' the sun was shinin' bright.

Did you, did you get that letter that I throwed in your backyard? Lord, Lord, Lord,
Did you get that letter that I throwed in your backyard?
It said I'd come to see you, but your best man's got me barred.

I'm gonna buy me a shotgun, long as I am tall, Lord, Lord, Lord,
Gonna buy me a shotgun, long as I am tall,
If she won't have me she won't have no man at all.

I'm goin' away baby, I won't be back till fall, Lord, Lord, Lord,
I'm goin' away baby, I won't be back till fall,
And if I find me a good girl, I won't be back at all.

Recommended versions on YouTube: Gertrude "Ma" Rainey ("See See Rider") Big Bill Broonzy, Elvis Presley.

Ma Rainey (1886-1939), the first professional blues singer to gain national recognition.

15

Careless Love

In this famous 16-bar blues, a downhearted woman bemoans getting pregnant due to "careless love." According to the New Orleans cornetist Joe "Wooden" Nicholas, it was composed by Buddy Bolden, the pioneering jazz trumpeter whom Jelly Roll Morton called "the blowingest man since Gabriel." The lyrics were first published in 1911 by Howard W. Odum in the *Journal of American Folklore*. Bessie Smith recorded a popular version in 1925 for Columbia that would greatly influence gospel singer Mahalia Jackson, and W. C. Handy published an arrangement of the song in 1926.

Traditional blues
Swing 8ths

Arr. G. Weiser

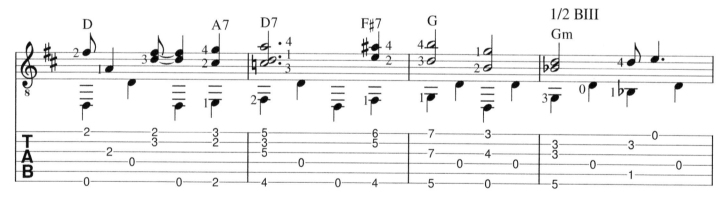

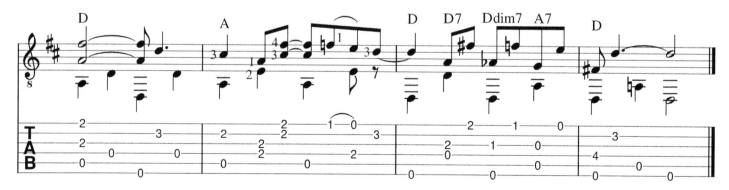

Careless Love

Love, oh love, oh careless love,
Love, oh love oh careless love,
Love , oh love oh careless love,
You see what careless love has done.

When I wore my apron low,
When I wore my apron low,
When I wore my apron low,
You'd follow me through rain and snow.

Now my apron strings won't pin,
Now my apron strings won't pin,
Now my apron strings won't pin,
You pass my door but you won't come in.

Careless love made me weep and moan,
Careless love made me weep and moan,
Careless love made me weep and moan,
It made me lose my happy home.

Careless love left my mother crying,
Careless love left my mother crying,
I'm going to shoot you and stand over you,
Until I see you finish dying.

(Repeat first verse)

Recommended versions on YouTube: Bessie Smith,
Big Walter Horton, Leadbelly, Blind Boy Fuller.

Bessie Smith in 1923. By 1922 she was a vaudeville prima donna with a considerable following before her first records were released. By the end of 1923 her popularity was that of a superstar.

Frankie and Johnny

This famous 12-bar blues is about an 1899 murder in St. Louis. Twenty-two year-old Frankie Baker shot her seventeen year-old lover, Allen Britt, when he returned home from a local dance hall after winning a slow dancing contest with a woman named Nellie Bly (not the journalist). The song has been recorded by many artists including Elvis Presley, Johnny Cash, Lena Horne, Sammy Davis Jr., Bob Dylan, and Charlie Poole.

Traditional blues

Arr. G. Weiser

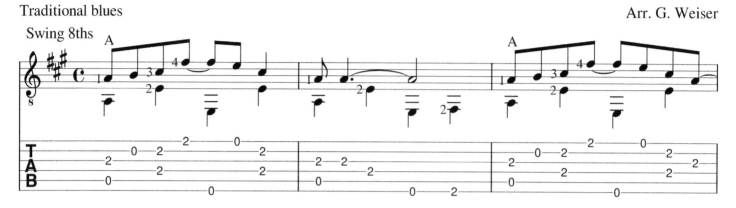

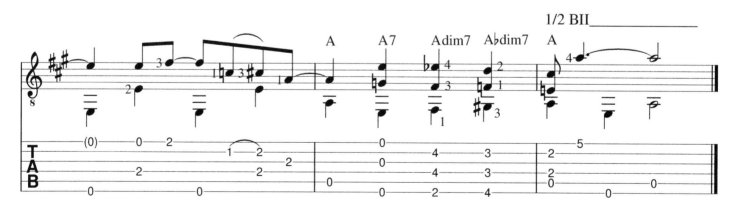

Frankie and Johnny

Frankie and Johnny were sweethearts, Lordy how they could love ,
They swore to be true to each other, true as the stars above,
He was her man, but he done her wrong.

Frankie she was a good woman, as everybody knows,
She spent one hundred dollars to buy Johnny a suit of clothes,
He was her man, but he done her wrong,

Frankie went down to the corner, just for a bucket of beer,
She said "Mister Bartender, has my loving Johnny been here?
He's my man, he wouldn't do me wrong."

"I ain't gonna tell you no stories, I ain't gonna tell you no lies,
Now I saw Johnny an hour ago with a gal named Nellie Bly,
He's your man, but he's doing you wrong."

Now Frankie looked over the transom, and she saw to her surprise,
There on the couch lay Johnny making love to Nellie Bly,
He was her man, but he was doing her wrong.

Frankie threw back her kimono, and drew out her forty-four,
Rooty toot-toot three times she shot and Johnny fell on the floor
She shot her man, he was doing her wrong.

"Bring out a hundred policemen, bring 'em around today,
To lock me in that jail cell and throw the key away,
I shot my man, he was doing me wrong."

Now Frankie she said to the warden, "What are they going to do?"
The warden he said to Frankie, "It's the electric chair for you,
You shot your man, he was doing you wrong,"

Now this story has no moral, this story has no end,
This story only goes to show that there ain't no good in men,
He was her man, but he done her wrong.

Recommended versions on You Tube: Jimmy Rodgers, Sam Cooke, Merle Haggard.

The Golden Vanity (Child 286)

An English ship at sea is menaced by an enemy vessel, variously described as Turkish, French, or Spanish. With promises of riches and his daughter's hand in marriage, the captain entices the cabin boy to swim to the side of the hostile warship and sink her by drilling holes in her. The wicked captain then betrays the boy, who in various versions drowns in the sea, is hauled up dead, or takes revenge and sinks The Golden Vanity.

Traditional English ballad

Arr. G. Weiser

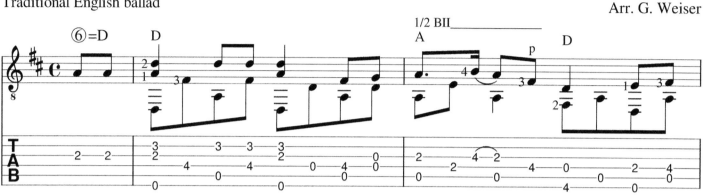

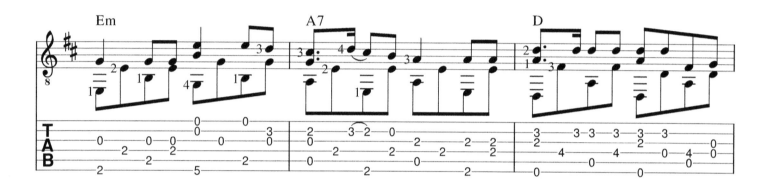

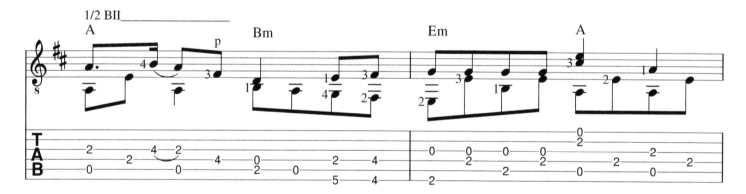

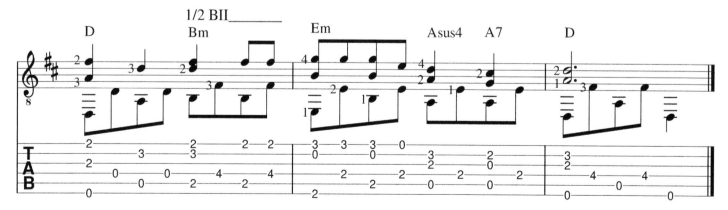

20

The Golden Vanity

Oh, there was a lofty ship and she sailed on the sea
And the name of the ship was the Golden Vanity,
But she feared she would be taken by a Turkish enemy,
As she sailed on the lowland, lowland, low,
She sailed upon the lowland sea.

Then up steps the cabin boy, just the age of twelve and three,
And he says to the captain, "What will you give to me,
If I swim alongside of your Turkish enemy,
And I sink her in the lowland, lowland, low,
I sink her in the lowland sea?"

"Oh I will give you silver and I will give you gold,
And the hand of my daughter if you will be so bold,
As to swim alongside of the Turkish enemy,
And to sink her in the lowland, lowland, low,
To sink her in the lowland sea."

Then the boy he made ready, and overboard jumped he,
And he swam alongside of the Turkish enemy,
And with his little drilling tool he bored holes three,
And he sank her in the lowland, lowland, low,
He sank her in the lowland sea.

Then the boy he turned around and back again swam he,
And he shouted for the captain to haul him from the sea,
But the captain would not heed, for his daughter he did need,
And he left him in the lowland, lowland, low,
He left him in the lowland sea.

Then the crew they hauled him out, but upon the deck he died,
And they wrapped him in his blanket so very soft and wide,
They cast him overboard to drift upon the tide,
And he sank beneath the lowland, lowland, low,
He sank beneath the lowland sea.

Oh, there is a lofty ship and she sails on the sea,
But she sails without a cabin boy the age of twelve and three,
and she fears she will be taken by a Turkish enemy,
As she sails on the lowland, lowland, low,
She sails on the lowland sea.

Recommended versions on YouTube: Peter, Paul and Mary, Burl Ives.

Jack Tar the Sailor

A sailor's life was often one of hardship, as the lyrics of this 18th-century broadside ballad attest. 'Jack Tar' was a common term during the British Empire for an English seaman, either of the merchant fleet or the naval line. The name likely derives from any of the various ways sailors used tar: to make their clothes waterproof, to coat the ropes of the rigging to prevent rot, or to use on their ponytails to keep their hair from getting tangled in the gear. The Byrds recorded this song on their 1969 album *The Ballad of Easy Rider*.

Sea shanty

Arr. G. Weiser

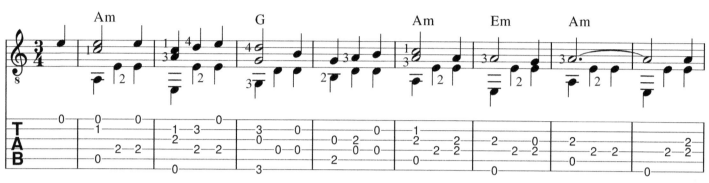

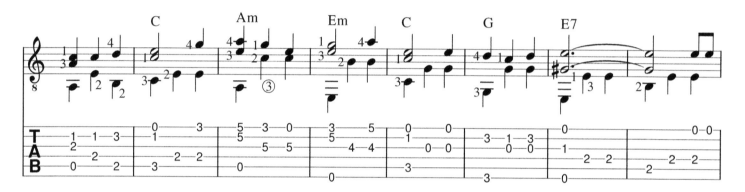

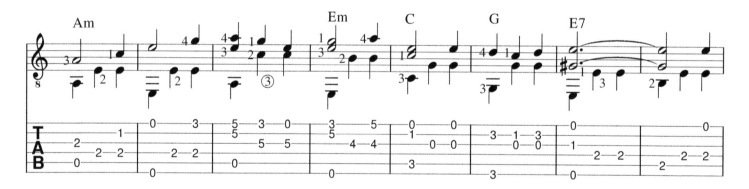

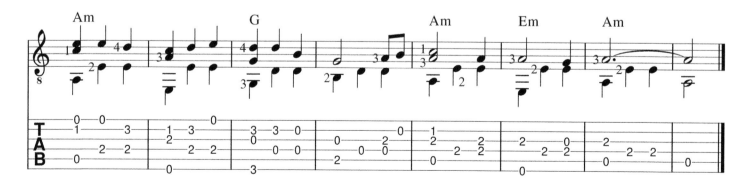

Jack Tar the Sailor

When first I came to Liverpool I went upon a spree,
Me money alas, I spent it fast, got drunk as drunk could be,
And when my money was all gone it was then that I wanted more,
But a man must be blind to make up his mind to go to sea once more.

I spent the night with Angeline too drunk to roll in bed,
Me watch was new and my money too and with them both she fled,
And as I roamed the streets about the whores they all would roar,
"There goes Jack Tar, that poor sailor, he must go to sea once more."

As I walking down the street I met with Rapper Brown,
I asked him for to take me on and he looked at me with a frown,
He said "Last time you was paid off with me you chalked no score,
But I'll take your advance and I'll give you a chance, and I'll send you to sea once more."

They shipped me aboard on a whaling ship bound for the Arctic Sea,
Where the cold winds blow through the frost and the snow, and Jamaica rum would freeze,
Alas I had no hard weather gear for I lost my money ashore,
It was then that I wished that I was dead and could go to sea no more.

Come all ye young seafaring lads and listen to my song,
And when you come off them long trips pray that you don't go wrong,
Take my advice drink no strong drink, don't go sleeping with no whores,
But get married, lads, and have all night in and go to sea no more.

Recommended versions on You Tube: The Byrds, Garcia and Grisman ("Off to Sea Once More"), Ewan Maccoll ("Off to Sea Once More"), The Dubliners ("Go to Sea No More").

Roger McGuinn- the Byrds.

John Barleycorn Must Die

This traditional English ballad is based on the ancient pagan belief in the annual death and resurrection of the Corn King, and was in print by 1635. Ironically, the many attempts to kill John Barleycorn narrated in the lyrics coincide with the process of growing, harvesting, and grinding barley for ale. Stevie Winwood learned the song from the British folk group The Watersons in 1965 and recorded a rock version with Traffic in 1970. This arrangement is a Travis picking approach to the tune.

Traditional English ballad

Arr. G. Weiser

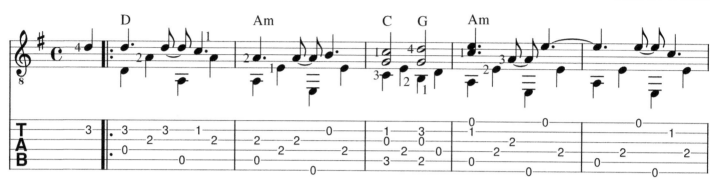

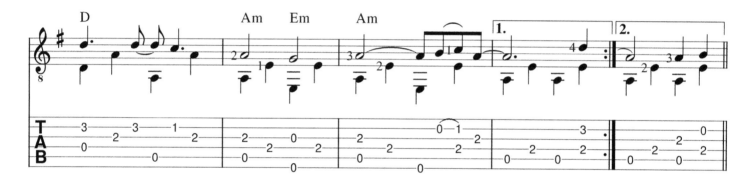

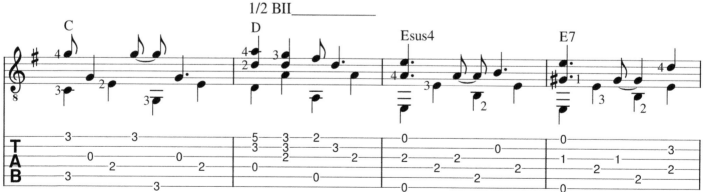

John Barleycorn Must Die

There were three men came out of the West,
Their fortunes for to try,
And these three men made a solemn vow:
John Barleycorn must die.
They've ploughed, they've sewn, they've harrowed him in,
Threw clods upon his head,
And these three men made a solemn vow,
John Barleycorn was dead.

They've let him lie for a very long time,
~Till the rains from heaven did fall,
And little Sir John sprung up his head,
And so amazed them all.
They've let him stand ~till midsummer's day,
~Till he looked both pale and wan,
And little Sir John's grown a long, long beard,
And so become a man.

They've hired men with the scythes so sharp,
To cut him off at the knee,
They've rolled him and tied him by the waist,
Serving him most barbarously.
They've hired men with the sharp pitchforks,
Who pricked him to the heart,
And the loader he has served him worse than that,
For he's bound him to the cart

They've wheeled him around and around the field,
~Till they came unto a barn,
And there they made a solemn oath,
On poor John Barleycorn.
They've hired men with the crab-tree sticks,
To cut him skin from bone,
And the miller he has served him worse than that,
For he's ground him between two stones.

And little Sir John and the nut-brown bowl,
And he's brandy in the glass;
And little Sir John and the nut-brown bowl,
Proved the strongest man at last.
The huntsman, he can't hunt the fox,
Nor loudly blow his horn,
And the tinker he can't mend kettle nor pot,
Without a little Barleycorn

Recommended versions on You Tube: Traffic,
Steeleye Span, Martin Carthy and Dave Swarbrick,
The John Renbourn Group.

John Henry

According to tradition, John Henry was a black raiload worker on the C&O line in the Big Bend Tunnel in West Virginia, which was completed in 1873. The legend goes that Henry, who could skillfully wield a sledgehammer to break up rock so dynamite could be placed for blasting, had a daylong contest with a steam-powered rock drilling machine. Although he won, he died of exhaustion soon afterwards. For years after Henry's death, many workers in the tunnel claimed to have heard or seen his ghost, sometimes with a hammer in each hand. Sounds of an unseen hammer would cause work stoppages, and recruiting workers got difficult. Guy Johnson collected the lyrics in 1900, and the song was often played as a slide guitar piece.

American folk song

Arr. G. Weiser

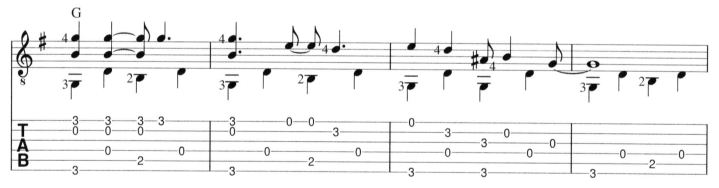

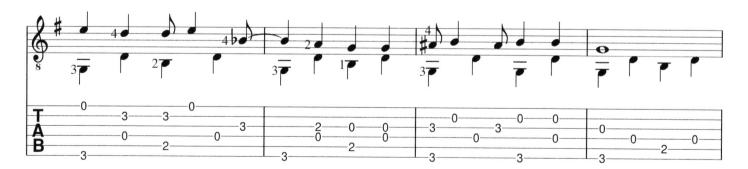

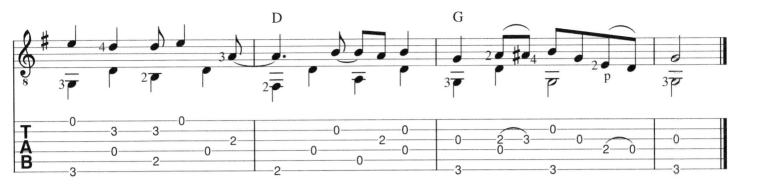

John Henry

When John Henry was a wee little boy,
Sittin' on his daddy's knee,
He picked up a hammer and a little piece of steel;
Said, "Hammer's gonna be the death of me, Lord,
Lord.
Hammer's gonna be the death of me."

The captain said to John Henry
"Gonna bring that steam drill 'round,
Gonna bring that steam drill out on the job.
Gonna whup that old steel on down, down, down.
Whup that old steel on down."

John Henry said to the captain,
"A man ain't nothin' but a man,
Before I let your steam drill beat me down,
I'll die with a hammer in my hand. Lord, Lord.
I'll die with a hammer in my hand."

John Henry said to his shaker,
"Shaker, why don't you sing?
I'm throwin' thirty pounds from my hips on down,
Just listen to that cold steel ring. Lord, Lord,
Listen to that cold steel ring."

The man that invented the stream drill,
Thought he was mighty fine,
But John Henry, he made fifteen feet;
The steam drill only made nine, Lord, Lord,
The steam drill only made nine.

John Henry hammered in the mountain,
His hammer was striking fire,
But he worked so hard, he busted his poor heart.
He laid down his hammer and he died, Lord, Lord,
He laid down his hammer and he died.

John Henry had a little woman,
Her name was Polly Ann,
John Henry took sick and went to his bed,
Polly Ann drove steel like a man, Lord, Lord,
Polly Ann drove steel like a man.

John Henry had a little baby,
You could hold him in the palm of your hand,
The last words I heard that poor boy say,
"My daddy was a steel-driving man, Lord, Lord,
My daddy was a steel-driving man."

In the tunnel, they have heard a hammer,
Swung by an unseen hand,
And the people they say, right to this very day,
It's the ghost of a steel driving man, Lord, Lord,
It's the ghost of a steel driving man.

Well, every Monday morning,
When the bluebirds begin to sing,
You can hear John Henry a mile or more,
You can hear John Henry's hammer ring, Lord,
Lord,
You can hear John Henry's hammer ring.

Recommended versions on You Tube: Woody
Guthrie and Cisco Houston, Tennessee Ernie Ford,
John Fahey, Bill Monroe.

The House Carpenter (Child 246)

In this traditional English ballad, the Devil appears to a married woman in the guise of an old lover and with promises of riches lures her away from her carpenter husband and baby. Out at sea she realizes her sin and tearfully laments it. The boat sinks and the pair go to Hell, where the adulteress is damned. The arrangement here is based on Joan Baez's version, and has been worked out with an alternating bass line.

English ballad

Arr. G. Weiser

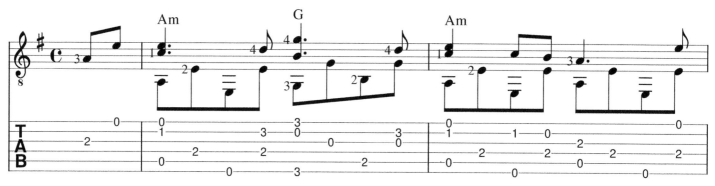

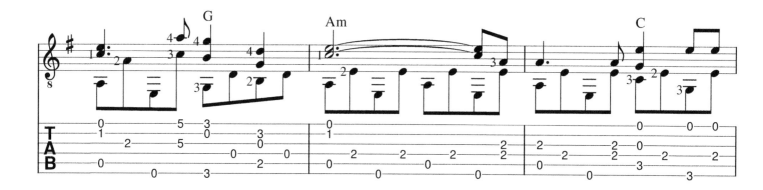

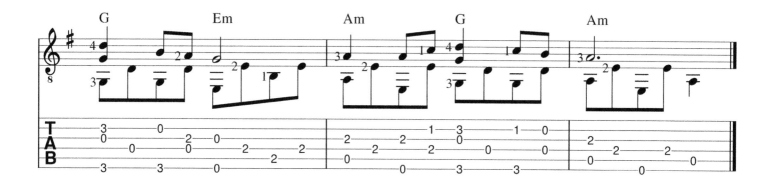

The House Carpenter

"Well met, well met, my own true love,
Well met, well met," cried he,
"I've just returned from the salt, salt sea,
All for the love of thee."

"I could have married the king's daughter dear,
She would have married me,
But I have forsaken her crowns of gold,
All for the love of thee."

"Well, if you could have married, the king's
daughter dear,
I'm sure you are to blame,
For I am married to a house carpenter,
And find him a nice young man."

"Oh, will you forsake your house carpenter,
And go along with me?
I'll take you to where the grass grows green,
To the banks of the salt, salt sea."

"Well, if I should forsake my house carpenter,
And go along with thee,
What have you got to maintain me on,
And keep me from poverty?"

"Six ships, six ships all out on the sea.
Seven more upon dry land,
One hundred and ten all brave sailor men,
Will be at your command."

She picked up her own wee babe
Kisses gave him three,
Said, "Stay right here with my house carpenter,
And keep him good company."

Then she put on her rich attire,
So glorious to behold,
And as she trod along her way,
She shown like the glittering gold.

Well, they'd not been gone but about two weeks,
I know it was not three,
When this fair lady began to weep,
She wept most bitterly.

"Ah, why do you weep, my fair young maid,
Weep it for your golden store?
Or do you weep for your house carpenter,
Who never you shall see anymore?"

"I do not weep for my house carpenter,
Or for any golden store,
I do weep for my own wee babe,
Who never I shall see anymore."

Well, they'd not been gone but about three weeks,
I'm sure it was not four,
Our gallant ship sprang a leak and sank,
Never to rise anymore.

One time around spun our gallant ship,
Two times around spun she,
Three times around spun our gallant ship,
And sank to the bottom of the sea.

"What hills, what hills are those, my love,
That rise so fair and high?"
"Those are the hills of heaven, my love,
But not for you and I."

'And what hills, what hills are those, my love,
Those hills so dark and low?"
"Those are the hills of hell, my love,
Where you and I must go."

Recommended versions on YouTube: Joan Baez,
Pentangle, Doc Watson.

Doc Watson and his son Merle in 1964.

The House of the Rising Sun

Many theories exist regarding the origins of this traditional song in which a woman laments a wayward life. According to the folksong collector Alan Lomax, "Rising Sun" occurs as the name of a bawdy house in two English ballads, and that the setting was relocated to New Orleans by southern planters. Evidence for an American origin, however, is a January 1821 *Louisiana Gazette* ad for the Rising Sun Hotel at 535 Conti Street touting "attentive servants." The large number of ladies' enamel-coated tin rouge pots found in the ruins of an 1822 fire there also suggests the establishment may have been a brothel. Also, in 19th-century New Orleans there was a dance hall called the The Rising Sun Hall, and a madam named Marianne LeSoleil Levant, whose surname means 'rising sun' in French. Alternatively, the folksinger Dave Van Ronk maintained that the song was about the Orleans Parish Women's Prison, which had a rising sun emblazoned on its gates, making the reference in the lyrics to the "ball and chain" literal. It was first recorded in 1933 by Clarence Ashley and Gwen Foster as "Rising Sun Blues." Later versions were waxed by Woody Guthrie, Leadbelly, Bob Dylan, and most famously, The Animals in 1964.

American folk song

Arr. G. Weiser

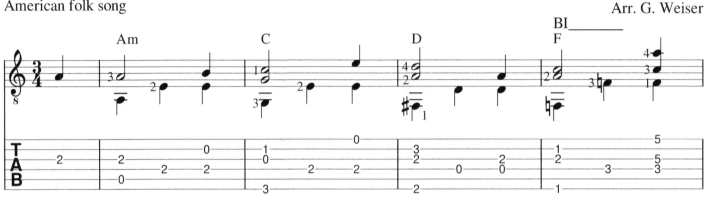

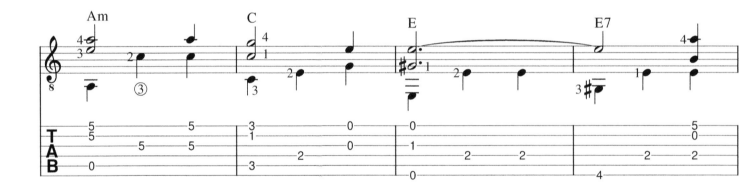

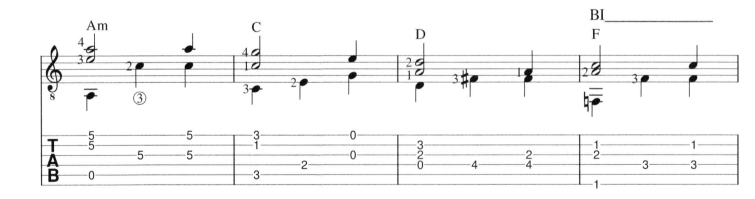

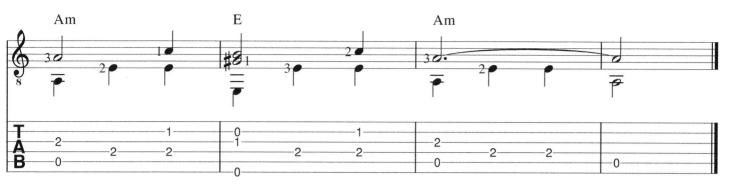

The House of the Rising Sun

There is a house in New Orleans,
They call the Rising Sun,
And it's been the ruin of many a poor girl,
And God, I know I'm one.

My mother was a tailor,
She sewed my new blue jeans,
My father was a gambling man,
Way down in New Orleans.

Now the only thing a gambler needs,
Is a suitcase and a trunk,
And the only time that he is satisfied,
Is when he's on a drunk.

He fills his glass up to the brim,
And passes the cards around,
And the only pleasure that he knows,
Is rambling from town to town.

Oh mothers, tell your children,
Not to do what I have done,
Spend your life in sin and misery,
In the House of the Rising Sun.

I got one foot on the platform,
The other on the train,
I'm going back to New Orleans,
To wear that ball and chain.

I'm going back to New Orleans,
My race is almost run,
I'm going back to end my days,
In the House of the Rising Sun.

Recommended versions on You Tube: The
Animals, Bob Dylan, Joan Baez, Dave Van Ronk.

Woody Guthrie and Leadbelly.

The Last Rose of Summer

The lyrics to this lovely Irish song were written in 1805 by the poet Thomas Moore in Co. Kilkenny, where he had been inspired by a specimen of Rosa 'Old Bush.' For the melody, Moore used the air "The Young Man's Dream," which Edward Bunting had collected in 1792 from the harper Denis Hempson at the Belfast Harp Festival. The song has been arranged by Beethoven, Mendelssohn, Gounod, Britten, and other composers.

Thomas Moore,
Traditional Irish air

Arr. G. Weiser

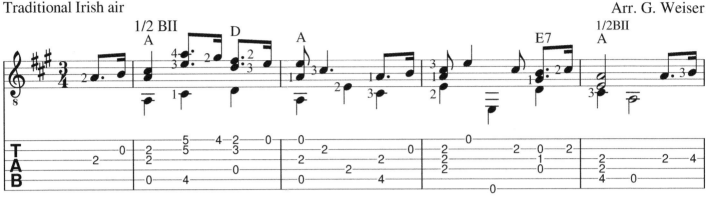

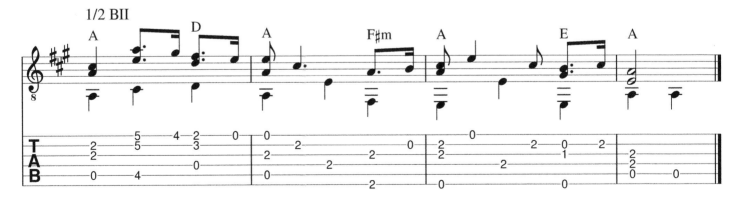

The Last Rose of Summer

'Tis the last rose of summer,
Left blooming alone,
All her lovely companions,
Are faded and gone,
No flower of her kindred,
No rosebud is nigh,
To reflect back her blushes,
And give sigh for sigh.

I'll not leave thee, thou lone one!
To pine on the stem,
Since the lovely are sleeping,
Go, sleep thou with them,
Thus kindly I scatter,
Thy leaves o'er the bed,
Where thy mates of the garden,
Lie scentless and dead.

So soon may I follow,
When friendships decay,
And from Love's shining circle,
The gems drop away,
When true hearts lie withered,
And fond ones are flown,
Oh! who would inhabit
This bleak world alone?

Recommended versions on YouTube: Renee
Fleming, Nina Simone, John McDermott.

Loch Lomond

The origins of this famous Scottish Jacobite song are unknown, but by one account it tells of two prisoners in Carlisle Castle after the Scottish defeat at Culloden in 1746. One will be freed to return home overland by the "high road," and the other, who is to die, by the "low road" - a fairy tunnel by which it was believed that souls of Celts who died outside of Scotland would be repatriated. Loch Lomond is a lake in southern Scotland.

Traditional Scottish song

Arr. G. Weiser

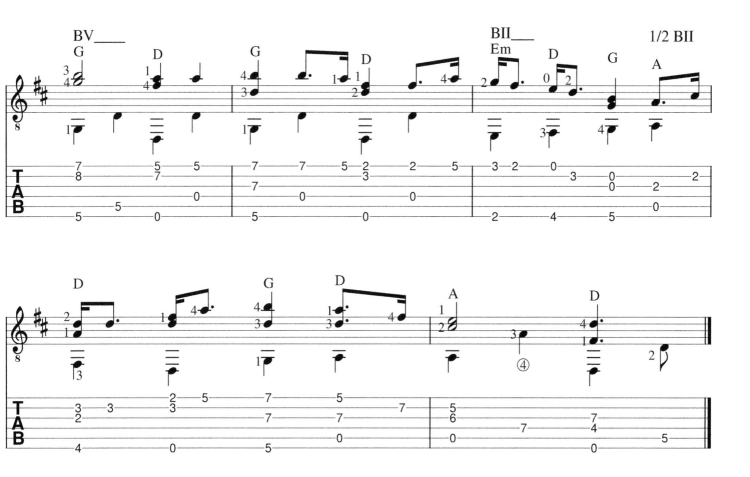

Loch Lomond

By yon bonnie banks and by yon bonnie braes,
Where the sun shines bright on Loch Lomond,
Where me and my true love were ever wont to go,
On the bonnie, bonnie banks of Loch Lomond.

Chorus:
O ye'll take the high road and I'll take' the low road,
An' I'll be in Scotland afore ye,
But me and my true love will never meet again,
On the bonnie, bonnie banks of Loch Lomond.

We'll meet where we parted in yon shady glen,
On the steep, steep side o' Ben Lomond,
Where in purple hue the Highland hills we view,
And the moon looks out from the gloamin'.
(chorus)

O brave Charlie Stuart! dear to the true heart,
Who could refuse thee protection,
Like the weeping birch on the wild hillside,
How graceful he looked in dejection!
(chorus)

The wild birdies sing and the wild flowers spring,
An' in sunshine the waters are sleepin',
But the broken heart it knows, no second spring,
Though the woeful may cease from their greetin'!
(chorus)

Recommended versions on You Tube: Robert Wilson, The Corries, Irish Roses.

Peggy-O

In this song a soldier seeks the hand of a lady, who despite her fondness for him, refuses him for his lower social standing. It traces back to a Scottish broadside ballad first published in 1839 called "The Bonnie Lass of Fyvie," and was collected by Cecil Sharpe in the southern Appalachians in the early 20th century as "Pretty Peggy-O." It has been recorded by Bob Dylan, Joan Baez, and most famously, the Grateful Dead. This arrangement is based on a May 11, 1977 performance by the Grateful Dead.

Traditional Scottish ballad

Arr. G. Weiser

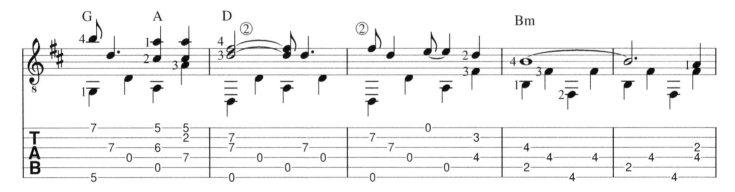

Peggy-O

As we rode out to Fennario,
As we rode out to Fennario
Our captain fell in love with a lady like a dove,
And called her by name, pretty Peggy-O.

Will you marry me pretty Peggy-O,
Will you marry me pretty Peggy-O,
If you will marry me, I'll set your cities free,
And save all the ladies in the are-o.

In a carriage you shall ride, pretty Peggy-O,
In a carriage you shall ride, pretty Peggy-O,
In a carriage you shall ride, with your true love by your side,
The fairest lady in the are-o.

I would marry you sweet William-O,
I would marry you sweet William-O,
I would marry you but your guineas are too few,
And I fear my mama would be angry-o.

What would your mama think pretty Peggy-O,
What would your mama think pretty Peggy-O,
What would your mama think if she heard my guineas clink,
And saw me at the head of my soldiers-o.

Come trippin' down the stairs pretty Peggy-O,
Come v down the stairs pretty Peggy-O,
Come trippin' down the stairs combin' back your yellow hair,
Bid a last farewell to your William-O.

If ever I return pretty Peggy-O,
if ever I return pretty Peggy-O,
If ever I return your cities, I will burn,
And destroy all the ladies in the area-o.

Sweet William is dead pretty Peggy-O,
sweet William is dead pretty Peggy-O,
Sweet William is dead and he died for a maid.
The fairest maid in the area-o.

As we rode out to Fennario,
As we rode out to Fennario,
Our captain fell in love with a lady like a dove,
And called her by name, pretty Peggy-O.

Recommended versions on YouTube: Grateful Dead, Joan Baez ("Fennario").

Scarborough Fair

Descended from the Scottish ballad "The Elfin Knight" (Child 2), this song uses the device of the riddle. A lady sets her suitor a series of seemingly impossible tasks, all ending with the refrain, "parsley, sage, rosemary, and thyme." In 1965 Paul Simon learned the song from the British folksinger, Martin Carthy, and with Art Garfunkel recorded it for the soundtrack of the 1967 film, *The Graduate.* Scarborough is a coastal resort town in North Yorkshire where an annual 45-day fair beginning in mid-August was held from 1253 to about 1750.

Traditional English ballad

Arr. G. Weiser

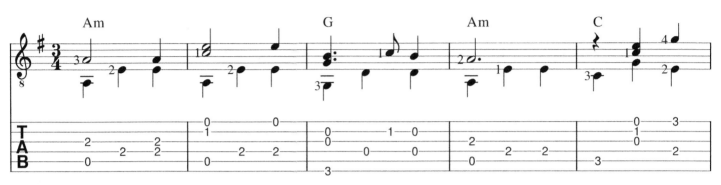

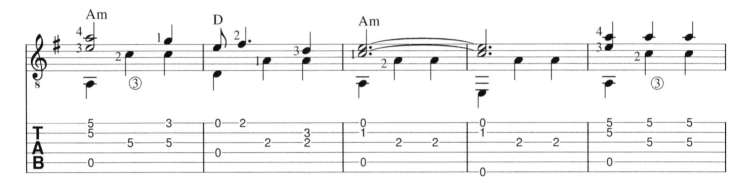

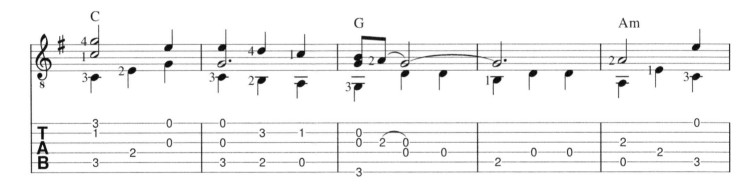

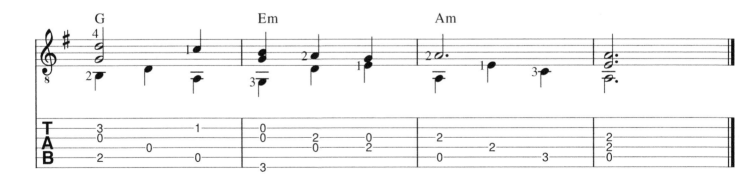

Scarborough Fair

Are you going to Scarborough Fair,
Parsley, sage, rosemary and thyme,
Remember me to one who lives there,
For she once was a true love of mine.

Have her make me a cambric shirt,
Parsley, sage, rosemary and thyme,
Without no seam nor fine needle work,
And then she'll be a true love of mine.

Tell her to weave it in a sycamore bower,
Parsley, sage, rosemary and thyme,
And gather it all with a basket of flowers,
And then she'll be a true love of mine.

Have her wash it in yonder dry well,
Parsley, sage, rosemary and thyme,
where water ne'er sprung nor drop of rain fell,
And then she'll be a true love of mine.

Have her find me an acre of land,
Parsley, sage, rosemary and thyme,
Between the sea foam and over the sand,
And then she'll be a true love of mine.

Plow the land with the horn of a lamb,
Parsley, sage, rosemary and thyme,
Then sow some seeds from north of the dam,
And then she'll be a true love of mine.

Tell her to reap it with a sickle of leather,
Parsley, sage, rosemary and thyme,
And gather it all in a bunch of heather,
And then she'll be a true love of mine,

If she tells me she can't, I'll reply,
Parsley, sage, rosemary and thyme,
Let me know that at least she will try,
And then she'll be a true love of mine,

Love imposes impossible tasks,
Parsley, sage, rosemary and thyme,
Though not more than any heart asks,
And I must know she's a true love of mine.

Dear, when thou has finished thy task,
Parsley, sage, rosemary and thyme,
Come to me, my hand for to ask,
For thou then art a true love of mine.

Recommended versions on YouTube: Martin
Carthy, Simon and Garfunkel.

The Sloop John B.

The sloop *John B.* was a 19th-century Bahamian sponger whose crew was known for revelry while ashore. Named for John Bethel, a Welshman who lived in the islands in the 1600s, she wrecked and sank at Governor's Harbor in Eleuthera around 1900. The song was collected in 1916 by Richard Le Gallienne and printed in *Harper's Weekly*. In 1966 The Beach Boys released a hit version as the lead single for their album *Pet Sounds*.

Bahamian folk song

Arr. G. Weiser

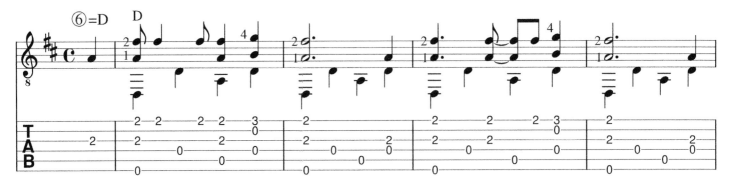

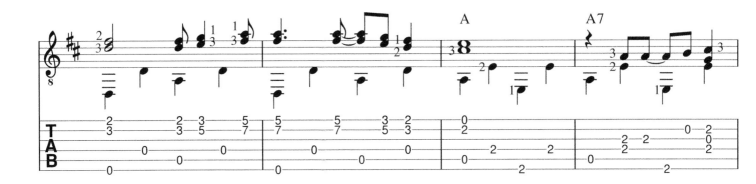

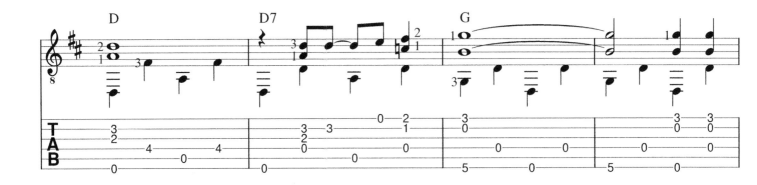

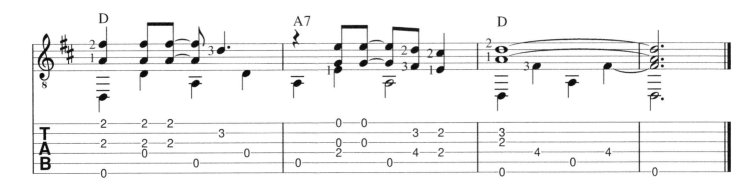

The Sloop John B

We sailed on the Sloop John B.,
My grandfather and me,
Around Nassau town we did roam,
Drinking all night,
Got into a fight,
Well I feel so broke up,
I want to go home.

Chorus:
So hoist up the John B's sail,
See how the main sail sets,
Call for the captain ashore,
Let me go home,
Let me go home,
I want to go home,
Well I feel so broke up,
I want to go home.

The first mate he got drunk,
And broke in the captain's trunk,
The constable had to come and take him away,
Sheriff John Stone,
Why don't you leave him alone,
Well I feel so broke up, I want to go home.
(chorus)

The poor cook he caught the fits,
And threw away all my grits,
And then he took and he ate up all of my corn,
Let me go home,
Why don't they let me go home,
This is the worst trip I've ever been on.
(chorus)

Recommended versions on YouTube: The Beach Boys, The Kingston Trio, Blind Blake Higgs.

St. James Infirmary

This 8-bar blues is believed to be descended from the English song "The Unfortunate Rake," which tells of a soldier who patronizes prostitutes and dies from venereal disease. The cowboy song "The Streets of Laredo" is another descendent. Evidence for a common ancestor is a song collected in 1918 in the southern Appalachians by Cecil Sharpe containing the lyric "As I went down by St. James Hospital one morning, so early one morning, it was early one day. I found my son, my own son, wrapped up in white linen, as cold as the clay." This New Orleans funeral dirge became famous when Louis Armstrong recorded it in 1928.

American blues

Arr. G. Weiser

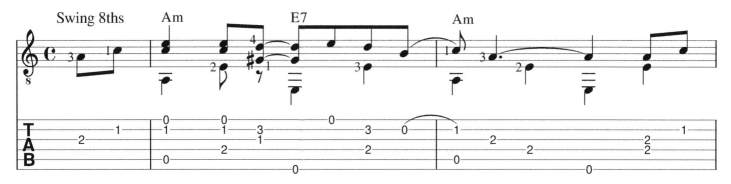

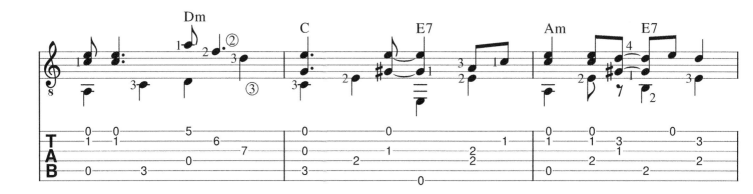

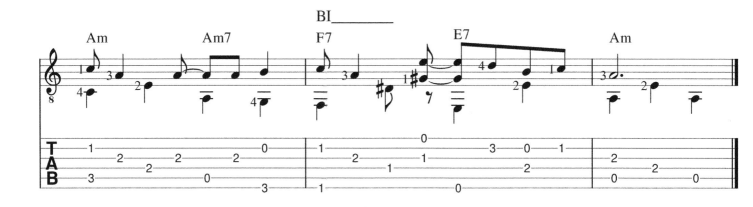

St. James Infirmary

It was down at old Joe's barroom,
On the corner by the square,
The drinks were served as usual,
And the usual crowd was there.

On my left stood old Joe McKennedy,
His eyes were bloodshot red,
He turned to the crowd around him,
These are the very words that he said.

I went down to St. James infirmary,
To see my baby there,
She was laid out on a long white table,
So young, so cold, so fair.

Let her go, let her go, God bless her,
Wherever she may be,
She may search this whole world over,
She'll never find another man as sweet as me.

When I die oh Lord please bury me,
In my high-top Stetson hat,
Put gold coins over my eyelids,
So the boys will know I died standing pat.

Get six gamblers to be my pallbearers,
Six chorus girls to sing me a song,
Put a jazz band behind my hearse wagon,
To raise hell as we roll along.

Get sixteen coal black stallions,
To pull that rubber-tired hack,
There's thirteen men going to the graveyard,
Bur only twelve men coming back.

Now that you have heard my story,
Let's have another round of booze,
And if anyone should ask you,
I've got those mean old gambler's blues.

(Repeat 3rd verse)

Recommended versions on YouTube: Louis Armstrong, Dave Van Ronk, Janis Joplin, Snooks Eaglin.

Shenandoah

In the early 19th century, the fur trappers who gathered pelts along the upper tributaries of the Mississippi sometimes took Native American wives. In this surpassingly beautiful folk song, a *voyageur*, as the traders were known, asks the Oneida chief Shenandoah (1710–1816) for his daughter's hand in marriage. The song spread down the Mississippi as a capstan sea shanty, and from there to sailors of clipper ships on the high seas.

Sea shanty

Arr. G. Weiser

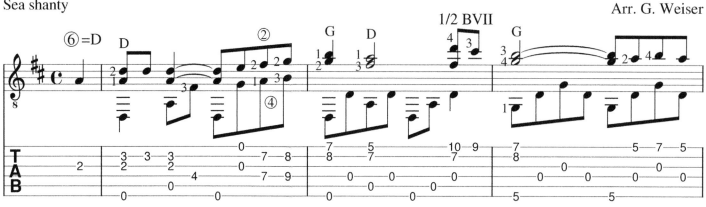

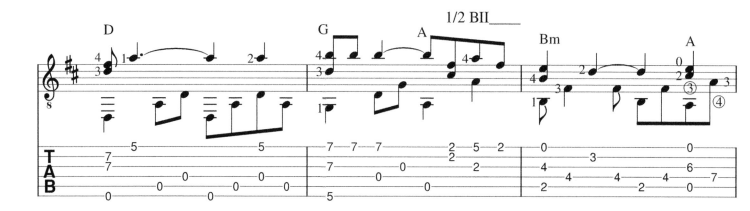

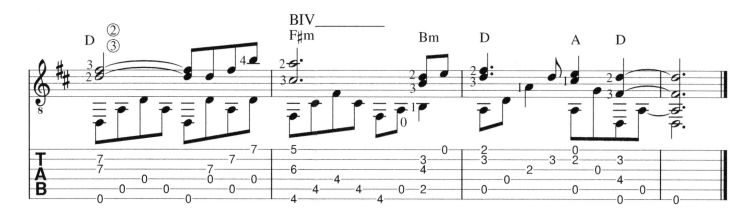

Shenandoah

Oh Shenandoah, I long to see you,
Away you rolling river,
Oh Shenandoah, I long to see you,
Away, I'm bound away 'cross the wide Missouri.

Oh Shenandoah, I love your daughter,
Away, you rolling river,
I'd cross for her your roaming waters,
Away, I'm bound away cross the wide Missouri.

'Tis seven years since last I've seen you,
Away, you rolling river,
Tis seven years since last I've seen you,
Away, we're bound away cross the wide Missouri.

Oh Shenandoah, I long to hear you,
Away you rolling river,
Oh Shenandoah, I long to hear you,
Away, I'm bound away 'cross the wide Missouri.

Recommended versions on YouTube: Sissel Kyrkjebo, Paul Robeson, John Kirk and Trish Miller, Glen Campbell.

Glen Campbell

The Water Is Wide

In this plaintive old Anglo-Scots ballad, also known as "Waly, Waly," a woman laments her mistreatment by an untrue lover. It is related to Child 204, "Jamie Douglas," which similarly tells of a Scottish lord's unhappy marriage. This is among the most beautiful folk melodies, and has been recorded by many famous singers. In this arrangement, bass arpeggios and other runs take up the slack created by the long notes in the treble.

Scottish folk song

Arr. G. Weiser

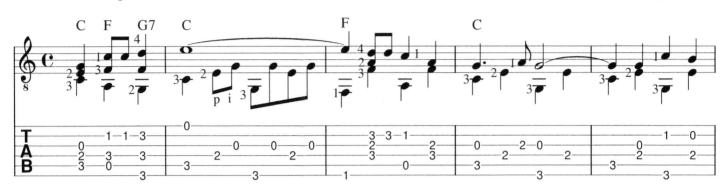

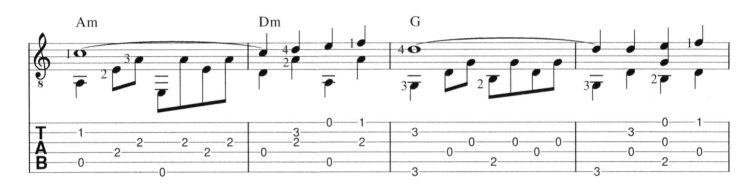

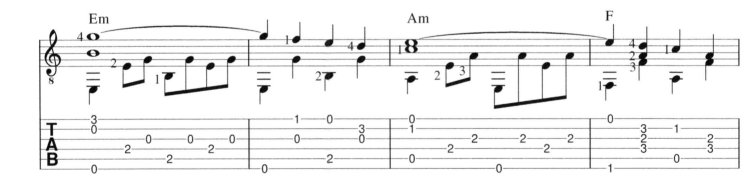

The Water is Wide

There is a ship and she sails the sea,
'Tis loaded deep as deep can be,
But not as deep as the love I'm in,
I know not how I sink or swim.

The water is wide, I cannot cross over,
And neither have I wings to fly,
Give me a boat that can carry two,
And both shall row my love and I.

I leaned my back up against an oak,
Thinking it was a trusty tree,
But first it bent and then it broke,
And so did my true love to me.

I reached my hand into some soft bush,
Thinking the fairest flower to find,
I pricked my finger to the bone,
And left the fairest flower behind.

Love is handsome and love is fine,
Bright as a jewel when first it's new,
But a love grows old and waxes cold,
And fades away like the morning dew.

When cockle shells turn to silver bells,
Then will my love come back to me,
When roses bloom in winter's gloom,
Then will my love return to me.

Recommended versions on YouTube: The Seekers, Joan Baez, Mary Hopkin, James Taylor

We Shall Overcome

This celebrated protest song was the anthem of the civil rights movement. Based on "I'll Overcome Some Day," a 1900 hymn by Charles Albert Tindley, it was later sung in labor movement, where folksinger Pete Seeger heard it in 1947. In 2018 a court voided a 1963 copyright claim by a group of songwriters including Seeger, and held the song to be in the public domain. It is arranged here in a choral style.

Charles Albert Tindley

Arr. G. Weiser

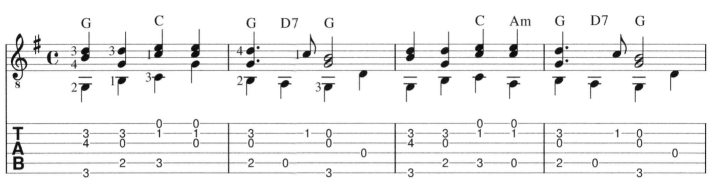

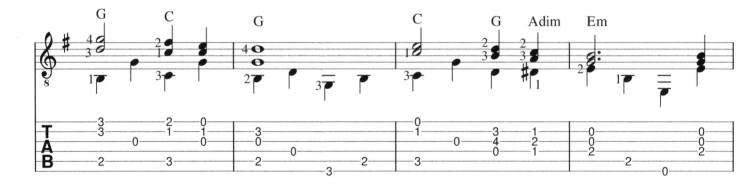

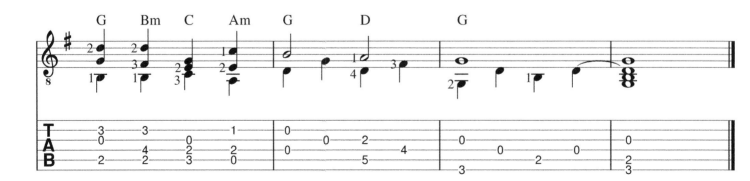

We Shall Overcome

We shall overcome, we shall overcome,
We shall overcome someday, someday,
Oh, deep in my heart, I do believe,
We shall overcome someday.

The Lord will see us through, the Lord will see us through,
The Lord will see us through someday, someday.
Oh, deep in my heart, I do believe,
The Lord will see us someday.

We're on to victory, we're on to victory,
We're on to victory someday, someday,
Oh, deep in my heart, I do believe,
We're on to victory someday.

We'll walk hand in hand, we'll walk hand in hand,
We'll walk hand in hand someday, someday,
Oh, deep in my heart, I do believe,
We'll walk hand in hand someday.

We are not afraid, we are not afraid,
We are not afraid today, today,
Oh, deep in my heart, I do believe,
We are not afraid today.

The truth shall make us free, the truth shall make us free,
The truth shall make us free someday, someday,
Oh, deep in my heart, I do believe,
The truth shall make us free someday.

We shall live in peace, we shall live in peace,
We shall live in peace someday, someday,
Oh, deep in my heart, I do believe,
We shall live in peace someday.

Recommended versions on YouTube: Pete Seeger, Joan Baez, Morehouse College.

Whiskey in the Jar

This rollicking ballad about a highwayman who robs a rich aristocrat traces back to the 17th century, when songs with Robin Hood-type heroes were popular, even if their protagonists were hanged in the end. This was sung in colonial America, and has been recorded by The Dubliners, Jerry Garcia, and even Metallica.

Traditional Irish folk song

Arr. G. Weiser

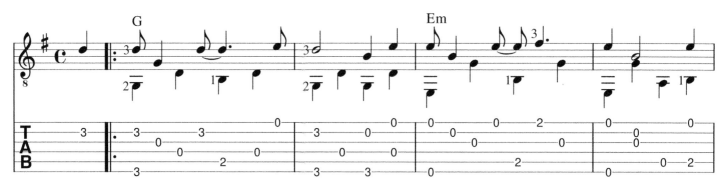

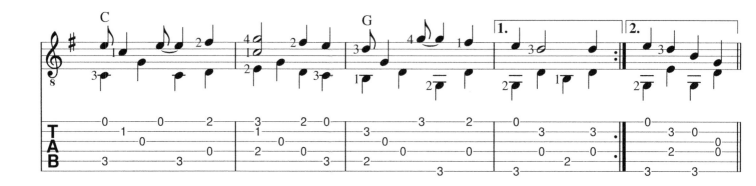

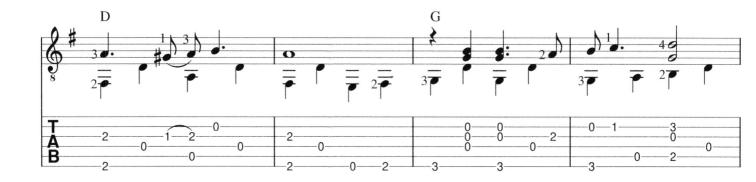

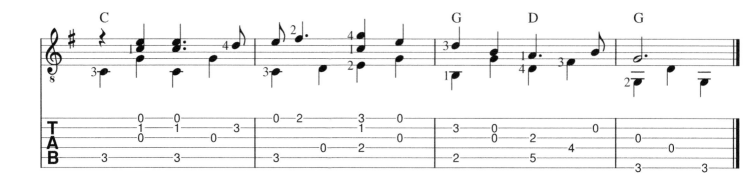

Whiskey in the Jar

As I was going over the Kilmagenny mountain,
I met with captain Farrell and his money he was countin',
I first produced my pistol, and then I drew my rapier,
I said stand by and deliver, for you are a bold deceiver.

Chorus:
Musha ring dumma do damma da,
Whack fol the daddy-o,
Whack fol the daddy-o,
There's whiskey in the jar.

I counted out his money, and it made a pretty penny,
I put it in my pocket and I brought it home to Jenny,
She said and she swore, that she never would deceive me,
But the devil take the women, for they never can be easy.
{chorus)

I went into my chamber, for to take a slumber,
I dreamt of gold and jewels and for sure it was no wonder,
But Jenny took my charges and she filled them up with water,
And send for captain Farrell to be ready for the slaughter.
(chorus)

It was early in the morning, before I rose to travel,
the guards were all around me and likewise captain Farrell,
I first produced my pistol, for she stole away my rapier,
But I couldn't shoot the water so a prisoner I was taken.
(chorus)

If anyone can aid me, it's my brother in the army,
If I can find his station in Cork or in Killarney,
And if he'll come and save me, we'll go roving near Kilkenny,
And I swear he'll treat me better than me darling sporting Jenny
(chorus)

Now some men take delight in the drinking and the roving,
But others take delight in the gambling and the smoking,
But I take delight in the juice of the barley,
And courting pretty Jenny in the morning bright and early.
(chorus)

Recommended versions on YouTube: The Dubliners, Garcia and Grisman, Metallica, Peter, Paul, and Mary ("Gilgarra Mountain").

Wildwood Flower

This song is thought to combine lyrical elements from an 1860 parlor song, "I'll Twine Midst the Ringlets" by Maude Irving and J. P. Webster, and "The Pale Amaranthus," a traditional Appalachian song. It evolved through the folk process before the Carter Family first recorded it in 1928. In 1942 Woody Guthrie borrowed the melody for his song "The Sinking of the Rueben James," and added a chorus to it.

American folk song

Arr. G. Weiser

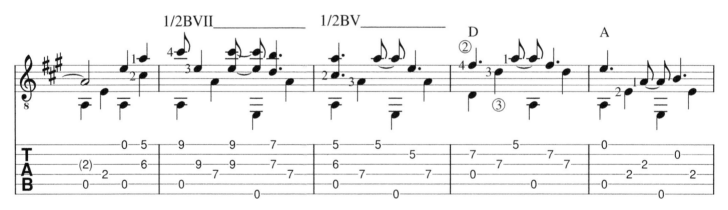

Wildwood Flower

I will twine and will mingle my waving black hair,
With the roses so red and the lilies so fair,
The myrtle so green of an emerald hue,
The pale amanita and violets of blue.

Oh, he promised to love me, he promised to love,
To cherish me always all others above,
I woke from my dream and my idol was clay,
My passion for loving had vanished away.

Oh, he taught me to love him, he called me his flower,
A blossom to cheer him through life's weary hour,
But now he has gone and left him alone,
The wild flowers to weep and the wild birds to moan.

I'll dance and I'll sing and my life shall be gay,
I'll charm every heart in the crowd I survey,
Though my heart now is breaking, he shall never know,
How his name makes me tremble, my pale cheeks to glow.

I'll dance and I'll sing and my life shall be gay,
I'll banish this weeping, drive troubles away,
I'll live yet to see him, regret this dark hour,
When he won and neglected his frail wildwood flower.

Recommended versions on YouTube: The Carter Family, The Kentucky Colonels, Emmylou Harris, Loretta Lynn.

The Carter Family, 1941.

Will the Circle Be Unbroken

In 1935 the Carter Family recorded this 1907 hymn by Ada R. Habershon and Charles H. Gabriel with reworked lyrics by A. P. Carter as "Can the Circle be Unbroken." The melody of the hymn was in turn taken from the spiritual "When I Lay My Burden Down." It has since become a country music anthem. The verses of the hymn, which are in the public domain, are given here.

American hymn

Arr. G. Weiser

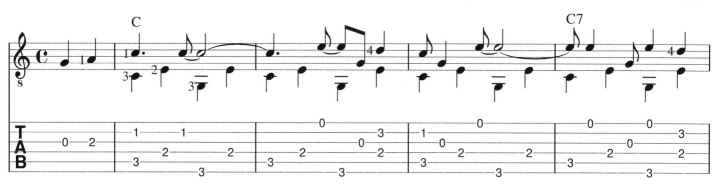

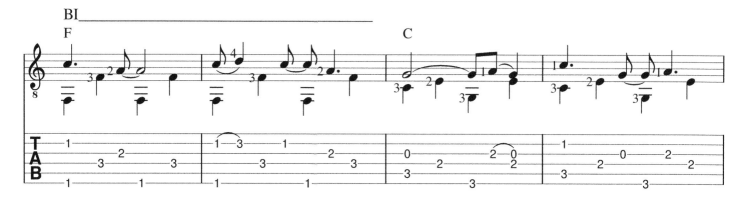

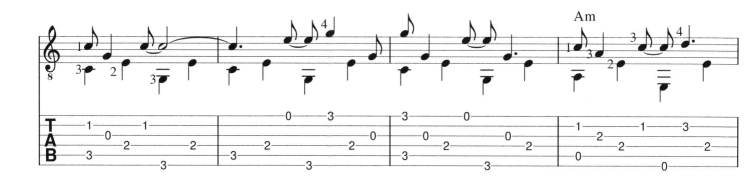

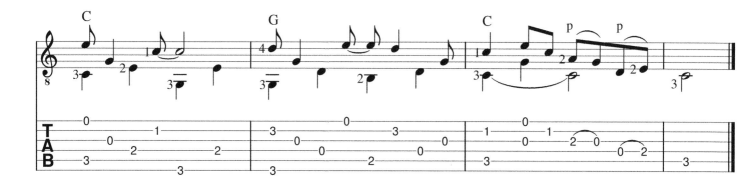

Will the Circle Be Unbroken

There are loved ones in the glory,
Whose dear forms you often miss,
When you close your earthly story,
Will you join them in their bliss?

Chorus:
Will the circle be unbroken,
By and by, by and by?
Is a better home awaiting,
In the sky, in the sky?

In the joyous days of childhood,
Oft they told of wondrous love,
Pointed to the dying Savior,
Now they dwell with Him above.
(chorus)

You remember songs of heaven,
Which you sang with childish voice,
Do you love the hymns they taught you,
Or are songs of earth your choice?
(chorus)

You can picture happy gatherings,
Round the fireside long ago,
And you think of tearful partings,
When they left you here below.
(chorus)

One by one their seats were emptied,
One by one they went away,
Now the family is parted,
Will it be complete one day?
(chorus)

Recommended versions on YouTube: The Carter Family, The Nitty Griity Dirt Band, The Staples Singers, George Jones.

More Great Guitar Books from Centerstream...

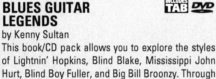